THE REALLY WICKED JOKE BOOK

THE
REALLY WICKED
JOKE BOOK

MICHAEL O'MARA BOOKS LTD

First published in Great Britain in 1998
by Michael O'Mara Books Limited
9 Lion Yard
Tremadoc Road
London SW4 7NQ

A CIP catalogue record for this book is available from the British Library

ISBN 1-85479-417-5

1 3 5 7 9 10 8 6 4 2

Cover design by Design 23

Designed and typeset by Design 23

Printed and bound by WSOY, Finland

REALLY WICKED DIRTY JOKES

Three men were on a trip to Saudi Arabia. One day, they came upon a harem with over 100 beautiful women. They started getting friendly with all the women, when suddenly the Sheikh came in.

"I am the master of all these women," he said, "No-one else can touch them except me. You three men must all pay for what you have done today. You will each die, but in the way that corresponds with your profession."

The Sheikh turned to the first man and asked him what he did for a living.

"I'm a police marksman," said the first man.

"Alright, shoot his penis off!" ordered the Sheikh.

He then turned to the second man and asked him what he did for a living.

"I'm a fireman," said the second man.

"Alright, burn his penis off!" ordered the Sheik.

Finally, he asked the last man, "And you, what do you do for a living?"

And the third man answered, with a big smile on his face,

"I'm a lollipop salesman!"

A man and a woman started to have sex in the middle of a dark forest. After 15 minutes of this, the man finally got up and said, "Damn, I wish I had a torch." The woman says, "So do I. You've been eating grass for the past ten minutes!"

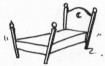

In the middle of his university course, a young man came to terms with his homosexuality and decided to come out of the closet. His plan was to tell his mother first; so, on his next home visit, he went to the kitchen, where his mother was busying herself stirring the stew with a wooden spoon.

Rather nervously, he explained to her that while he was at university, he had realized he was gay.

Without looking up from her stew, his mother said,

'You mean, you're homosexual?'

'Well...yes.'

Still without looking up: 'Does that mean you have other men's cocks in your mouth?'

Caught off guard, the young man eventually managed to stammer an embarrassed affirmative.

His mother turned to him and, brandishing the wooden spoon threateningly under his nose, snapped:

'Right! Don't you EVER complain about my cooking again!'

The stages of a woman's life:

Below the age of 14, she is like Antarctica: untouchable.

Between the ages of 14 and 17, she is like Africa: virgin and unexplored.

Between the ages of 18 and 30, she is like Asia: hot and exotic.

Between the ages of 30 and 45, she is like America: fully explored, breathtakingly beautiful and free with her resources.

Between the ages of 46 and 56, she is like Europe: exhausted but still with points of interest.

After 56, she is like Australia: everybody knows it's down there, but nobody gives a damn.

There was this bar in need of a piano player, so the manager hung a 'Piano Player Wanted' sign in the window. An hour or so later, a man walks in and asks to audition. The manager tells him to go ahead and play something. The man sits down and begins to play the greatest music the manager has ever heard.

Tears are welling up in his eyes as the man ends the song. The manager tells the man that it was the best thing he's ever heard and asks for the name of the song.

The man says, "I wrote that song. I call it 'Two guys having sex'." The manager winces, but before he can say anything, the man starts to play an even more beautiful song.

This time, when he ends, the manager is weeping.

Wiping away a tear, he tells the man that it was the loveliest song he's ever heard.

The man says, "I wrote that song too. I call it 'Six guys having sex with one really fat chick'."

The manager winces again but arrives at a solution.

He tells the man the job is his, but he must never tell the customers the names of the songs. The man understands and agrees to start the next night at 9:00 pm.

The next night, 9:00 pm rolls around and the man hasn't shown up. At 9:05 he comes charging through the door with his dress shirt unbuttoned, his flies open and his cock hanging out of his trousers. He races over to the piano and proceeds to play the most beautiful music anyone has ever heard. The manager calls one of his waitresses over and tells her to tell the man that his flies are undone and his cock is showing. The waitress makes her way over to the man and whispers in his ear, "Do you know your flies are open and your cock is sticking out?"

The man replies, "Know it, I wrote it!"

The other day we all went to this club. One of the guys wanted to impress us, so he pulled out a £10 note. The nude dancer came over to us, and my friend licked the £10 note and put it on her backside. Not to be outdone, my other friend pulled out a £50 note. He called the girl back over, licked the £50 note and stuck it on her other cheek.

Now all the attention was focused on me. What could I do to top that? I got out my wallet, thought for a minute – then the financial genius in my soul took over.

I got out my cash card, swiped it down her crack, grabbed the £60 and went home.

A woman walks into her accountant's office and tells him that she needs to complete her tax return.

The accountant says, "Before we begin, I'll need to ask a few questions." He gets her name, address and national insurance number, etc. and then asks, "What is your occupation?"

The woman replies,
"I'm a whore."
The accountant baulks
and says, "No, no, no.
That will never do.
That is much too crass.
Let's try to rephrase
that."
The woman says,
"Okay then, I'm a
prostitute."
"No, that is still too
crude. Try again."
They both think for a
minute, then the
woman states,
"I'm a chicken
farmer."
The accountant asks,
"What does chicken
farming have to do
with being a whore or
a prostitute?"
"Well, I raised over
5,000 cocks last year."

The Seven Most Important Men in a Woman's Life

1. The Doctor – who tells her to "take off all your clothes".

2. The Dentist – who tells her to "open wide".

3. The Milkman – who asks her "do you want it delivered to the front or the back?"

4. The Hairdresser – who asks her "do you want it teased or blown?".

5. The Interior Designer – who assures her "once it's inside, you'll love it!".

6. The Banker – who insists to her "if you take it out too soon, you'll lose interest!".

7. The Primal Hunter – who always goes deep into the bush, always shoots twice, always eats what he shoots, but keeps telling her "keep quiet, and lie still!".

There was a young lady from Ealing
Who professed to lack sexual feeling
Till a lady named Doris
Just touched her clitoris
And she had to be scraped off the ceiling.

QUESTIONS, QUESTIONS!

Q. Why did the gay man put sunflower seeds up his ass?
A. Because gerbils have to eat too.

Q. What do blondes say during sex?
A. "Are you all on the same team?"

Q. Why are blondes so quiet when they have sex?
A. They don't talk to strangers.

Q. Why do blondes wear underwear?
A. To keep their ankles warm.

Q. How does a blonde turn on the lights after having sex?
A. She opens the car door.

Q. What does a blonde put behind her ears to attract men?
A. Her ankles.

Q. Why did the condom fly across the room?
A. Because it got pissed off.

Q. Why don't debutantes like gang-bangs?
A. Too many thank-you notes to write.

Q. What's the difference between a clitoris and a pub?
A. Men can always find a pub.

Q. Why doesn't Santa Claus have any children?
A. Because he only comes once a year.

Q. What's the worse thing about oral sex?
A. The view.

Q. Why do mutes masturbate with only one hand?
A. So they can moan with the other.

Q. What's the difference between condoms and coffins?
A. They both hold something stiff but one's coming and one's going!

Q. Why does Barbie never get pregnant?
A. Because Ken always comes in a box!

Q: What is the difference between ooh and aah?
A: About three inches.

Q. What's the Ultimate Rejection?
A. When you're masturbating, and your hand falls asleep.

Q. Why do women still like to have a man around?
A. Because vibrators can't mow the lawn.

MECHANICAL AIDS

A businessman was going on a long business trip. He knew his wife was very flirtatious, so he thought he'd try to get her something to keep her occupied while he was gone, because he didn't like the idea of her having sex with someone else.

He went to a shop that sold sex toys and started looking around. He thought about the life-sized sex doll, but he thought it was too similar to a real man.

He started browsing through the dildos next, looking for something special to please his wife, and started talking to the old man behind the counter. He explained his situation.

The old man said, "Well, I don't really know of anything that will do the trick. We have vibrating dildos, special attachments, and so on, but I don't know of anything that will keep her occupied for weeks, except ," and he stopped.

"Except what?" the man asked.

"Nothing, nothing."

"Come on, tell me! I need something desperately!"

"Well, sir, I don't usually tell people about this, but there is the 'voodoo dick'."

"So, what is this voodoo dick?" the man

asked. The old man reached under the counter, and pulled out a wooden box, carved with strange symbols.

He opened it, and there lay a very ordinary-looking dildo.

The businessman laughed, and said, "Really! It looks like every other dildo in this shop!"

The old man replied, "But you haven't seen what it'll do yet." He pointed to the door and said, "Voodoo dick, the door!"

The voodoo dick rose out of its box, darted over to the door, and started having sex with the keyhole. The whole door shook with the vibrations, and a crack developed down the middle. Before the door looked like it was going to split in half, the old man said,

"Voodoo dick, box!" The voodoo dick stopped, floated back to the box and lay there, quiescent once more.

"I'll take it!" said the businessman. The old man demurred, saying it really wasn't for sale, but he finally surrendered it for £500 in cash.

The man took the dildo home to his wife, told her it was a very special dildo and that to use it, all she had to do was say "Voodoo dick, my pussy!"

He left for his business trip satisfied that everything would be fine while he was gone. After he'd been gone a few days, the wife was feeling unbearably sexy. She thought of several people who would willingly satisfy her, but then she remembered the voodoo dick. She got it out, and said, "Voodoo dick, my pussy!"

The voodoo dick immediately started having sex with her. It was amazing, like nothing she'd ever experienced before. After three orgasms, she decided she'd had enough, and tried to pull it out, but it was stuck inside her, still carrying on. She tried and tried to get it out, but nothing worked. Her husband had forgotten to tell her how to shut it off.

So she decided to go to the hospital to see if they could help. She put her clothes on, got in the car and started to drive to the hospital, quivering with every thrust of the dildo.

On the way, a violent orgasm nearly made her swerve off the road, and she was pulled over by a policeman. He asked for her licence, and then asked how much she'd had to drink.

Gasping and twitching, she explained that she hadn't been drinking, but that a voodoo dick was stuck inside her, and wouldn't stop having sex with her.

The officer looked at her sceptically, and then said:

"Yeah, right......... Voodoo dick, my ass!"

When he passed her bedroom, a father saw his daughter having sex with the aid of a vibrator.

"What on earth are you doing?" he said.

"Well, dad! I'm 30 years old, fat, ugly and I've never even had a boyfriend. There's no way I'll ever get married, so this electronic device is my substitute husband," replied the daughter.

Several days later, the daughter came home from work and saw her dad sitting in a chair, watching television.

He had a beer in one hand and her vibrator in the other.

"What's going on?" she asks.

"I'm just having a beer with my son-in-law," he said.

Some time ago, there was a man who went to Vietnam and got his arm blown off in a major battle. He went back to the United States a year later and talked to an old friend about his troubles. His friend told him about a new invention. The invention was a mechanical arm that did everything you told it to do.

The man was a little nervous about the idea but he decided to have a go with it. So a month later he got the mechanical arm attached and returned home for the first time.

He got to the front door and said, "Open the door!" The arm opened the door for him.

Then he said, "Close the door." The arm closed the door.

Later on that evening he was watching T.V. and wanted a beer, so he walked to the fridge and said, "Open the refrigerator and take me out a beer." The arm opened the door and got him a beer.

The man was delighted with the arm. About an hour later he was desperate for a piss. He went to the bathroom and said, "Unzip my flies and take my cock out."

The arm did as instructed, the man had a piss and, when he'd finished, he said, "Shake it a bit." The arm obeyed.

Well, he thought that felt quite good, so he said,

"Shake it again, harder." Well, he thought, that felt really good, so he said, "Jerk me off." The arm then proceeded to pull his cock off. The man screamed "Oh, f**k me." Then the arm put it up his rear. The man roared, "Oh, I can't believe what I'm seeing!"

So the arm shoved his cock in his eye.

WEDDED BLISS

A wife was cleaning out the wardrobe and right at the top of the top shelf she notices a large box. She carefully takes the box down and notices a sign on it which reads: DO NOT OPEN!

Naturally she was curious, so she opened the box and inside she found £10,000 in cash and three golf balls.

Later that evening her husband came home, and she immediately confronted him about the contents of the box.

The husband was very upset, but his wife asked, "Why are there three golf balls in the box?"

"Every time we had bad sex I put a golf ball in the box," the husband replied.

"Hmm, three golf balls, 20 years of marriage, that's not bad," she thought.

"So what's the £10,000 for?," she asked.

"Every time I got a dozen golf balls, I sold them."

First woman: "I never made love to my husband before we got married. How about you?"

Second woman: "I don't know. What's his name?"

On her wedding night, the young bride took her mother aside and said, "Ma, tell me how to make my new husband happy."

Her mother replied, "Well, when two people love each other, they make love."

"Oh, I know all about that, Ma," the bride responded. "I want to know how to make lasagne."

A man came home from work one day and gave his wife a dozen yellow roses. The next day, his wife was hanging out the washing in the back garden, and chatting to her neighbour over the fence.

"Yesterday", she said, "the old man gave me a dozen yellow roses, and now I suppose he expects me to lie on my back with my legs in the air for a week!"

"Why?" replied the neighbour, "don't you have a vase?"

A newly wed couple went to bed early on Christmas night.

The wife woke up in the middle of the night,

shook her husband awake and said: "Darling, Darling, wake up! I had the most amazing dream!"

Husband: "What? What was it?"

Wife: "In my dream I saw a Christmas tree that was decorated with lots of different kinds of cocks. There were big ones, small ones, black ones, white ones, and at the top of the tree was the most perfect one: it was really long and thick!"

Husband: "But of course, it was my cock, wasn't it?"

Wife: "No, it was John Parker's!"

The husband, annoyed that his wife had woken up him to tell him that she'd had a dream about John Parker's cock, rolled over and went back to sleep.

Later he woke up, shook his wife and said:

"Dearest, I had the most amazing dream!"

Wife: "What was it?"

Husband: "In my dream I saw a Christmas tree that was decorated with lots of different kinds of pussys. There were tight ones, loose ones, black ones, white ones, and at the very top of the tree was the perfect pussy: it was so tight and sweetly shaped!"

Wife: "Well, it must have been mine!"

Husband: "No, dearest! yours was holding the tree up!"

A man and his wife had been stranded on a desert island for many years. One day another man was washed up on shore. He and the wife were very attracted to each other right away, but realized that certain protocols must be observed.

The husband, however, was very glad to see the second man there. "Now we will be able to have three people doing eight hour shifts in the watchtower, rather than two people doing 12-hour shifts." The new man was only too happy to help out and volunteered to do the next shift. He climbed up the tower and began standing watch.

Soon the husband and wife started placing stones in a circle to make a fire to cook supper. The second man yelled down, "Hey, no sex down there!" They yelled back, "We're not having sex!"

A few minutes later they started to put driftwood into the stone circle. Again the second man yelled down, "Hey, no f**king!"

Again they yelled back, "We're not f**king!"

Later they were putting palm leaves on the roof of their shack to patch leaks. Once again the second man yelled down, "Hey, I said no sex!" They shouted back, "We're not having sex!"

Finally his shift was over so the second man climbed down from the tower and the husband climbed up to take his turn on watch. He wasn't even halfway up before the wife and second man are having passionate sex.

The husband looked down from the tower and said to himself, "My God! From up here it really DOES look as though they're f**king."

The man and woman had been married for quite a time. One day the husband, thinking he was being funny, grabbed his wife's boobs as she was getting into the shower and said to her,

"You know, if these were really firm, you wouldn't need a bra!" The wife became angry; it was such a horrible thing to say. The next day, as she was getting out of the shower, he grabbed her bottom and said,

"You know, if this was really firm, you wouldn't need a girdle!" Now the wife was really angry and started plotting her revenge.

The next day, as her husband was getting out of the shower, she grabbed his cock and said, "You know, if this was really firm I wouldn't need your brother!"

Jane was a first -time contestant on a quiz show, where you have to answer questions to win the cash prize.

Lady luck had smiled on her, so Jane had gained a substantial lead over her opponents. She even managed to win the game but, unfortunately, time ran out before the show's host could ask her the final £100,000 question.

Needless to say, Jane agreed to return the following day. She was nervous and fidgety as her husband drove them home.

"I've just got to win tomorrow," she said, "I wish I knew what the answers are. I'm not going to be able to sleep at all tonight. I will probably look terrible tomorrow."

"Relax, dear," her husband, Mike, reassured her,

"It will all be OK."

Ten minutes after they arrived home, Mike

grabbed the car keys and started heading for the door.

"Where are you going?" Jane asked.

"I have a little errand to run. I should be back soon," he replied.

Jane waited impatiently for Mike's return. After an agonizing three-hour absence, Mike returned, sporting a very wide and wicked grin. "Honey, I managed to get tomorrow's question and answer!" he exclaimed.

"What is it?" she cried excitedly.

"OK. The question is 'What are the three main parts of the male anatomy?' And the answer is 'The head, the heart, and the penis."

Shortly after that, the couple went to sleep, and Jane, now feeling confident and at ease, plummeted into a deep and restful slumber.

At 3:30 in the morning, however, Jane was shaken awake by Mike, who was asking her the big quiz show question. "The head, the heart, and the penis," Jane replied groggily before returning to sleep. And Mike asked her again in the morning, this time as Jane was brushing her teeth. Once again, Jane answered correctly.

Jane was once again was sitting on the set of the quiz show. Even though she knew both the question and answer, she could feel the butterflies in her stomach and terror running through her veins. The cameras started rolling and the host, after reminding the audience of the previous day's events, faced Jane and asked the big question.

"Jane, for £100,000, what are the main parts of the male anatomy? You have 10 seconds."

"Hmm, uhm, the head?" she said nervously.

"Very good. Six seconds."

"Eh, uh, the heart?"

Very good! Four seconds."

"I, uhh, oooooohh, darn! My husband drilled it into me last night and I had it on the tip of my tongue this morning..."

"That's close enough," said the game show host,"

CONGRATULATIONS! You have won £100,000."

A married man gets home early from work and hears strange noises coming from the bedroom. He rushes upstairs to find his wife naked on the bed, sweating and panting.

"What's up?" he asks.

"I'm having a heart attack," cries the woman.

He rushes downstairs to grab the phone, but just as he's dialling, his 4-year-old son comes up and says,

"Daddy! Daddy! Uncle Ted's hiding in your closet and he's got no clothes on!" The man slams the phone down and storms upstairs into the bedroom, past his screaming wife, and rips open the wardrobe door. Sure enough, there is his brother, totally naked, cowering on the closet floor.

"You bastard!" says the husband. "My wife's having a heart attack, and all you can do is run around the house naked scaring the kids?"

A woman was in bed, having sex with her husband's best friend when all of a sudden the telephone rings and she answers.

After hanging up she says, "That was Harry, but don't worry, he won't be home for a while. He's playing cards with you."

An escaped convict broke into a house and tied up a young couple who had been sleeping in the

bedroom. As soon as he had a chance, the husband turned to his voluptuous young wife, bound up on the bed in a skimpy nightgown, and whispered,

"Honey, this guy hasn't seen a woman in years. Just cooperate with anything he wants. If he wants to have sex with you, you just go along with it and pretend you like it. Our lives depend on it."

"Dearest," his wife hissed, spitting out her gag, "I'm so relieved you feel that way, because he just told me he thinks you have a really cute looking ass."

A husband and wife were in the bathroom getting ready to go to work when the husband looked at his wife and said, "I've just got to have you right now!"

He backed her up against the bathroom door, pulled down her knickers and had sex with her.

When they had finished, he started putting his clothes back on and saw his wife still writhing around against the door.

He asked, "What's wrong, honey? Didn't you come? Do you want more?"

His wife said, "No, no, it's not that. I'm just trying to get the door knob out of my behind"

Two men were discussing the new secretary at their office.

John said to George, "Man, I went out with her last Tuesday and we had wonderful sex. She's a lot better in bed than my wife!" Two days later, George said to John, "Well, I went out with her too and we had sex as well, but she certainly isn't that much better than your wife."

One night, a flying saucer lands in Dallas, Texas, in the back garden of a fun-loving married couple called Bob and Pat. A male and female alien emerge from the flying saucer and introduce themselves as being from Mars. They tell Bob and Pat that they came to Earth for an experiment. Tim asked, "What do you want from us?"

The aliens replied that they wanted to see what it was like to have sex with an earthling, and if the two of them would like to participate in their experiment. Bob and Pat thought it over and agree to give it a go. Bob took the female into one bedroom, while Pat took the male into another bedroom. As soon as the male alien was undressed, Pat looked at him and started laughing. The alien asked, "What's so funny?"

Pat replied, "I'm sorry, I shouldn't have laughed, but I just don't think you're large enough to satisfy any woman here on Earth!"

The alien replied, "No problem, watch this." He pulled on his ears and his cock quickly grew to ten inches.

Pat smiled and said, "Now, that's more like it!"

A few hours later, after the aliens had gone back to Mars, Bob asked Pat, "Did you enjoy sex with the alien OK, dear?"

"It was fantastic," replied a very happy Pat. Pat then returned the question, "How about you dear – did you enjoy sex with your alien?"

"It was fine," Bob replied, I just wish she'd stop pulling on my ears, though!"

There were these two Americans who played golf together every Saturday. Well, one Saturday they were getting ready to tee off when a guy on his own asked if he could join them.

The friends looked at each other and then looked at the man and said it was OK. So they teed off.

About two holes into the game, the friends got curious to know what the man did for a living. So they asked him. The stranger told them that he was a hit-man. The friends kind of laughed. The man said, "No really, I am a hit-man. My gun is in my golf bag. I carry it everywhere I go. You can take a look if you like."

So one of the men decided he would. He opened up the bag and, sure enough, there was this rifle with a huge telescopic sight on it. He got all excited about it. He said, "WOW! I bet I can see my house through this! May I look?"

The stranger handed him the rifle. The man looked through the sight and said, "YEAH! You can! I can even see through my windows into my bedroom. There's my wife, naked. Isn't she beautiful? WAIT THOUGH! There's my next door neighbour! He's naked too!" This so upset the man that he asked the hit-man how much it would be to do a hit.

The hit man replied, "It's $1000 every time I

pull the trigger."

The man said, "$1000, WOW! Well, OK. I want two hits. I want you to shoot my wife right in the mouth. She is always nagging at me and I can't stand it. Second, I want you to shoot my neighbour right in the cock, just for screwing around with my wife."

The hit-man agreed so he sets the gun up and looks through the scope. He was looking steadily for about 5 minutes. The man started to get impatient and asked the hit-man what he was waiting for. The hit-man replied,

"Just hold on a second... I'm about to save you a thousand bucks."

REALLY WICKED GOLF JOKES

Golfer: "This is a terrible golf course. I've never played on a worse one."

Caddie: "But this isn't the course! We left that more than an hour ago."

Phil and Tony had arranged a game of golf at the club. When they met up at the first tee, Phil was surprised to see Tony standing there with not one but two caddies by his side. They teed off and were about half-way around the course when Phil could not contain his curiosity any longer.

"What's this then?" asked Phil. "Did you win the lottery or something?"

"What do you mean?" asked Tony.

"You know what I mean," said Phil. "The two caddies. Why are you using two caddies?"

"Oh, them," said Tony. "My wife was complaining I wasn't spending enough time with the kids."

Golfer: "I've never played this badly before."

Caddie: "You've played before?"

Golfer: "That can't be my ball, caddie. It looks far too old."

Caddie: "It's a long time since we started, sir."

Golfer: "What a disastrous round. You must be the worst caddie in the world!"

Caddie: "I doubt it, sir. That would be too much of a coincidence!"

After a series of disastrous holes, the strictly amateur golfer, trying to smother his rage, laughed hollowly and said to his caddie: "This golf is a funny game."

"It's not supposed to be," said the caddie gravely.

A well known pro golfer hits his drive deep into the woods for the third time that day.

"The number four axe I think," he says with aplomb while turning to his caddie.

"I'd move heaven and earth to be able to break 100 on this course," sighed the elderly golfer.

"Try heaven,"advised his caddie, "You've already moved most of the earth.

The man was standing in the witness box of a court. "Have you ever taken the oath?" asked the judge. Then, noting the quizzical look on the man's face, added, "Do you know how to swear?"

"Oh yes, sir," he replied, "I'm your caddie."

The golfer and his caddie had been out on the course for what seemed like forever. After more than several hours had passed, the caddie began spending what, to the golfer, seemed to be an inordinate amount of time looking at his watch. The man was becoming annoyed at his caddie's actions and finally spoke up.

"I just want you to know," said the man, "that I'm aware that I'm not the world's greatest golfer. But even so, I've taken the whole day off work and I'm just going to relax and enjoy myself, no matter how long it takes to finish. So you can stop constantly looking at your watch."

"I fully appreciate that, sir," said the caddie, "but this is not my watch, it's a compass."

Few people carry a heavy burden further than golf caddies.

Colin was having a dreadful game and just seemed incapable of hitting the ball right. The caddie was teetering towards breaking point and it finally came after forty strokes or so at the sixth hole.

"What should I take for this one?" Colin asked innocently.

"Beats me," growled the caddie. "Seems like a toss up between a cyanide capsule or the next train out of town!"

The hacker came upon a hole that was famously said to possess the world's largest fairway bunker. Naturally, his tee shot, as if drawn by a magnet, found its way right into the heart of this monster. As they reached the abyss, the hacker peered over the edge and turned to his caddie.

"What club do you suggest?" he asked.

"Well, sir, it doesn't really matter much," the caddie replied, "but may I suggest that you don't go in there without an adequate supply of food and water."

The miserly old skinflint met up with his caddie, who he rather resented having to employ, at the first tee. The caddie placed his bag down and handed him his driver.

"Before we head out," cracked the old guy, "I want to know something. How good are you at finding lost balls?"

"As it happens, sir," replied the caddie, "I take great pride in my ability to find lost balls."

"Well then, what are you waiting for?" snapped the old guy. "Get out there and find one so we can get going!

"Look, that's it!" said the exasperated golfer to his insolent young caddie. "I've had enough of your cheek and I'm going to report you to the caddie master as soon as we get back to the clubhouse."

"Yeah, yeah," responded the youth, "I'm really worried now."

"You should be worried." said the golfer.

"Oh yeah, why's that?" said the youth. "At the rate you play, by the time we get back it'll be time for me to retire anyway."

After hitting his tee shot deep into the woods, the hacker turned to his caddie.

"Did you see where that one went to?" he asked.

"No, sir, as a matter of fact I didn't." replied the caddie.

"Why on earth didn't you watch where it went?" snapped the angry golfer.

"Frankly, sir," said the caddie, "I was totally unprepared for it to go anywhere."

The lady golfer was a determined, if not very proficient player. At each swipe she made at the ball, earth flew in all directions.

"Goodness me," she exclaimed red-faced to her caddie, "the worms will think there's an earthquake."

"Oh, I don't know," replied the caddie, "the worms round here are very clever. I expect most of them are hiding underneath the ball for safety."

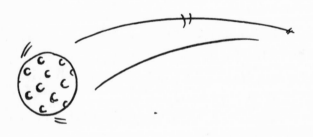

DOCTOR
DOCTOR

His doctor told him to play thirty – six holes a day, so he went out and bought a harmonica.

A dentist was right in the middle of working on a patient when the phone rang. Picking it up he listened for half a minute and then said,

"Yes, yes, I see. Don't worry, I'll be right over." Hanging up the phone, he quickly removed his mask and gloves, went over to a cupboard, grabbed his golf clubs and rushed out of the office. "Good heavens, Doctor," exclaimed his astonished nurse, "What's happened? Where are you going?"

"It's an emergency!" replied the dentist, as he raced through the door. "I have eighteen cavities to fill!"

A man was brought in to the accident and emergency department of a major London hospital one day, almost at death's door. He had somehow managed to get a golf ball lodged deep in his throat. He was immediately rushed into an operating room where a dedicated team of surgeons and throat specialists tried to save his life by removing the ball. After some tense hours the surgery was over and the operation was declared a complete success. The chief surgeon came out into the waiting room to find a man anxiously pacing up and down with three overflowing ashtrays beside him.

"Are you a member of the family?" the doctor asked him.

"No," replied the man, "But it's my ball."

First man: "My doctor has told me I can't play golf."

Second man: "So he's played with you too, has he?"

When the Maharajah of Merchandani was taken suddenly ill during a holiday in England, he was attended by a young locum filling in for the Harley Street surgeon. The Maharajah's appendix was deftly removed and the patient was overjoyed.

"You have saved my life," he said to the young man. "Whatever you want shall be yours."

"It was quite simple really," protested the young doctor.

"But I am a very rich man, I insist," said the princely patient.

"Well, I would love a new set of matched golf clubs," the young doctor admitted.

"Consider it done," came the stately reply.

Several weeks went past and the doctor had forgotten all about this grand promise until one day he received this cable:

"HAVE YOUR CLUBS BUT SADLY ALL NOT MATCHED STOP FOUR DO NOT HAVE SWIMMING POOLS STOP."

"God dammit, George, you surely don't expect me to pay that?" The two golfers were discussing a bill that George, the hospital administrator, has sent to Richard, a recent father for the first time.

"I mean, George, £35 for the use of the delivery room. It's just not on, old chap. You know I didn't get the wife there in time and the baby was born on the hospital's front lawn."

George leant over, took the bill, crossed out the offending entry and substituted another.

"Greens Fee, £35," it read.

Kevin loved playing golf but he had one small problem: every time he stood over a short putt he became flatulent. The weird thing was that whenever he became flatulent it would sound exactly like the word 'Honda.'

One day he went to Japan on a business trip and, following a successful meeting, he was invited to play a round of golf with his Japanese associates. Although he felt rather nervous because of his problem, it would have been insulting to refuse and so he accepted.

Sure enough, on the very first green, his problem became evident, and, as usual, it sounded just like 'Honda.' Overcome with embarrassment, Kevin began to apologise, when one of his partners said, "No need to worry – we can give you the name of a doctor in Tokyo who will be able to help you."

The following day he visited the doctor in Tokyo who, after being told of the nature of the problem, said, "Just get up onto the examination table here. I'm sure I can fix you right up."

After a lengthy examination the doctor exclaimed, "Ah, I know what your problem is – you have an abcess."

"What on earth does an abcess have to do with my condition?" asked Kevin.

"Don't you know?" said the doctor, "Abcess makes the fart go Honda!"

An elderly gentleman golfer lived on the third floor of a retirement home, next to the golf club. He used the path across the course as a short cut to the supermarket each day. One day, he was returning from the supermarket with a paper carrier full of groceries when he saw a stack of brand new golf balls beside the path. Unable to resist temptation, he emptied out his groceries and filled the bag. Unfortunately the ground was wet where the sprinklers were watering the greens and the damp paper burst, spilling the balls. Patiently he collected them all up and stuffed his pockets with them. As he waited for the lift, back at the retirement home a lady stood beside him and looked curiously at his bulging pockets.

Embarrassed, the old boy mumble, "Golf Balls," by way of explanation.

"Oh my," said the lady "Is that like tennis elbow?"

A golfer was taken to hospital suffering from sunstroke. The nurse began to read his temperature: "102 – 103 – 104 –"
"Hey, Doc," whispered the patient. "What's par for this hospital?"

REALLY
WICKED
IRISH
JOKES

Two Irish nuns, Sister Mary Magdalen and Sister Mary Joseph, are driving back to the convent in their ancient Morris Minor, when suddenly a vampire bat lands on the bonnet of the car and sits there looking through the windscreen at them.

"Jesus, Mary and Joseph!" exclaims Sister Mary Magdalen. "Will ya look at that! We've got to do something about that evil creature! Show it yer cross, Sister!"

So Sister Mary Joseph winds down her window, leans out and shouts, "Get off my bloody bonnet!"

An Irishman was on board a plane waiting to take off to Dublin when a rumour began amongst all the passengers that the Pope was going to be on the same flight. The man was a staunch Catholic who revered the Pope and he was thrilled and amazed when the Holy Father was seated right next to him. He tried his best to keep cool and leave the Pope in peace, but he couldn't help noticing that the Pope was doing a crossword puzzle and seemed to be having some difficulty finishing it.

Suddenly the Pope turned to the Irishman and said, "Are you any good at crossword puzzles, my son? I'm having problems with this one."

The Irishman was overwhelmed by the fact that not only was he sitting next to the Holy Father, but also that he was being engaged in conversation by him. "Well I'm very fond of crosswords as it happens, perhaps I can help you," he answered.

"Oh good," said the Pope. "Can you think of a four letter word describing a woman that ends in 'UNT'?"

The Irishman was silent for a few moments

and then, looking relieved, said, "Yes, I have it: 'AUNT'."

"Thank you!" said the Pope. "Now, could you lend me a rubber?"

The priest and the minister found that they frequently travelled on the same bus together although, of course, they never exchanged a word. Eventually the minister decided that it would be a Christian act to break the silence and he said, "Good day, Father Curran. We seem to see each other rather often and I feel we really should be on speaking terms – after all, we're both in the same business, are we not?"

"Indeed we are," replied the priest. "But you're doing it your way and I'm doing it His!"

Early one morning in rural Ireland, a group of leprechauns knocked on the door of the convent and demanded to see the Mother Superior. When she came out they all stood there looking at her, in silence. So finally she said, "How can I help you?" at which one of the leprechauns stepped forward and asked,

"Mother Superior, are there any wee little leprechaun nuns here in this convent?"

Somewhat startled, the Mother Superior replied, "No, there aren't any wee little leprechaun nuns in this convent."

"Well then," continued the spokesman, "Are there any wee little leprechaun nuns in county Waterford?"

Confused, the Mother Superior said, "No, there are no wee little leprechaun nuns in county Waterford."

"Let me ask you one last question, then," said the leprechaun, "Do you know of any wee little leprechaun nuns in any convent, in any county in all of Ireland?"

Totally bewildered now, the Mother Superior answered, "I know of no wee little leprechaun nuns in any convent, in any county in the whole of Ireland."

The leprechauns all turned to one another, smiling and whispering, and gradually they got louder and louder until the Mother Superior finally heard what they were saying: "Paddy f**ked a penguin! Paddy f**ked a penguin!"

It was the stockbroker's first day in prison and on meeting his violent-looking Irish cell mate, he became even more nervous than ever.

"Don't worry, mister," said the prisoner, noticing how scared the stockbroker was looking, "I'm in for a white collar crime, too."

The stockbroker sat down on his bunk, weak with relief. "Thank goodness!" he said. "What was it you did?"

"Oh," the prisoner replied. "I murdered a priest."

Four Irish nuns go out for a weekend. On Monday they come back and need to confess their sins. The first nun goes into the confessional and says, "Bless me, Father, for I have sinned. I touched a penis with this finger."

"You are forgiven," the priest replies. "Just swirl your finger in the holy water."

The second nun goes in. "Bless me, Father, for I have sinned. I fondled the private parts of a man with this hand."

And the priest says, "You are forgiven, Sister, just clean off your hand in the holy water."

The third nun was about to go into the confessional when the fourth nun says, "Sister Mary Patrick, please may I go in ahead of you? Otherwise I'll be drinking what you sit in."

An Irish Catholic went to confession. "Bless me, Father, for I have sinned. I had sex with a married woman."

"That is a mortal sin," the priest says. "You must tell me who she was."

"I can't do that, Father," the man replies. "It wouldn't be right."

"Was it Mary Stephens?"

"No."

"Was it Tricia O'Mara?"

The man shakes his head and says, "Please, Father, don't try to make me tell."

"If you won't tell me, then your penance will be fifty Hail Marys and fifty Our Fathers."

The priest sends the man away. Outside, he sees his friend, who's been waiting for him and who asks, "Did you tell him?"

"Yes."

"And what did you get?"

"Fifty Hail Marys, fifty Our Fathers and a couple of great tips."

An Irish priest meets a rabbi and they start to chat. "Tell me, Rabbi, have you ever eaten pork?" asks the priest.

"Well," replies the rabbi, "I once gave in to temptation and ate a ham sandwich. If we're exchanging special confidences, let me ask you something important: have you ever been with a woman?"

The priest looks sheepish but replies, "Yes, once, two years ago. I was at the end of my tether and tried the services of a prostitute in my parish."

"And what did you think of it?" enquires the rabbi.

"It beats the hell out of a ham sandwich," the priest replies.

In Ireland today, all the young girls stay out all night sowing their wild oats. And in the morning you can find them in church, praying for a crop failure.

Mary O'Donahue was eighty years old and a devout Catholic. Every day she walked the two miles to attend Mass at the local church, and every Friday she went to confession. She had followed this routine all her life. One Friday she went in to the confessional and said," Bless me, Father, for I have sinned. I have committed adultery with a seventeen-year-old gardener's boy."

The priest was absolutely horrified. "Good heavens, Mary O'Donahue, and when was that?"

"Oh, a good fifty years ago, Father, but I felt like recalling some pleasant experiences this week."

Why are so many Irish priests alcoholics?
Because they are drawn to the pure in spirit.

Deirdre Conlan was talking to the village priest at the end of Mass, and the priest said, "You know, Deirdre, I pray for you every night."

"Well, there's really no need to, Father, I am on the phone," she replied.

THE
SPORTING
IRISH

Did you hear about the Irish sky diver?

He was killed when his snorkel and flippers failed to open.

Brendan McCann walked into his local fishmonger's early one morning and asked to buy half a dozen trout. "Certainly, Brendan." the fishmonger replied, and started to wrap them.

"No, no!" Brendan exclaimed. "Please don't wrap them up. Can you just throw them to me gently, one by one?"

"Well, I can, but why on earth would you want me to do that?" asked the fishmonger. "You see," Brendan replied, "I've been out fishing the stream all night long without a sniff of a bite and if you throw those trout to me and I catch them, I can honestly tell Molly when I get home that I caught six trout."

The great Irish game hunter was stalking in the jungles of Africa, when he stumbled across a beautiful woman, lying naked in a clearing.

"Begorrah!" he said, "Are you game?"

She gave a seductive smile and said, "Why, yes, I am!"

So he shot her.

Two Irishmen bought themselves a horse each and decided to keep them in the same field.

"How shall we tell which horse is which?" Paddy asked Sean.

"I'll tie a green ribbon to my horse's tail," replied Sean.

Unfortunately, the ribbon on Sean's horse fell off one day in his absence, so the two of them were again faced with the problem of deciding which horse was which.

"I know!" said Paddy. "You have the brown horse and I'll have the white one."

A young Irishman walks into a chemist's shop and asks for a box of tampons. The sales assistant is surprised and says, "Young man, what do you want with tampons?"

"Well," says the young man, "my sister says that if you use them, you can run, go horseback riding, and take part in all kinds of dangerous sports."

Did you hear about the Irish skier with frost-bite on his bottom?

He couldn't figure out how to get his trousers over his skis.

A German bobsleigh team was competing in the Winter Olympics. Suddenly there was a terrible crash. The German team met the Irish team coming up.

THE

DEMON

DRINK

Two old Irish drunks were drinking in the pub together, when the first one says: "You know, Mick, when I was 30 and got a hard-on, I couldn't bend it with both hands. When I was 40, I could bend it about 10 degrees if I tried really hard. By the time I was 50, I could bend it about 20 degrees, no problem. I'm 60 next week and now I can almost bend it in half with just one hand."

"So," says the second drunk, "What's your point?"

"The point is, I'm just wondering how much stronger I'm going to get."

Old Dolan always was nosy. When the new neighbours moved in next door, he stood by the window and studied every piece of furniture that went into the place. There wasn't much, only a load of beer barrels.

"Begorrah, Mabel," he called out. "They're having the place nicely furnished next door."

Tim was on holiday in Ireland, staying at a small country pub. One evening he was amazed to overhear the following conversation:

"That's a beautiful hat you've got there," said an old boy to a young fellow who was standing next to him at the bar. "Where did you buy it?"

"At O'Grady's," replied the young man.

"Why, I go there myself," commented the old boy. "You must be a local chap then?"

"Aye, I am – from Murphy Street."

"Well, by all the saints, what a coincidence!" exclaimed the old boy. "That's where I'm from too!"

"That's amazing," said Tim to the barman, "That those two people live in the same street and have only just met."

"Don't you believe it!" said the barman. "They're actually father and son but they're always too drunk to recognize each other!"

A drunk staggered into Limerick churchyard and fell asleep amongst the tombstones. Early the next morning he was woken by the sound of a local factory hooter and, seeing where he was, concluded, not unnaturally, that he had heard Gabriel's trumpet. "Boy, oh boy," he said to himself, "Not a soul risen but me! This speaks badly for Limerick."

Did you hear about the queer Irishman?
  He preferred women to whiskey.

There was an old club man in St. Stephen's Green who always drank his whiskey with his eyes closed. When he was asked to explain his strange habit, he said, "It's like this: whenever I see a glass of whiskey my mouth waters, and I don't care to dilute it."

Paddy was taking a short-cut home through the fields one night after leaving the pub, when he thought he heard a little voice saying, "Help, please help me!" Peering about, he could see no-one but starting off on his way, he heard the voice again. This time he had a good search around and finally found a little leprechaun with his foot caught in a trap. Paddy carefully freed the leprechaun who said, "I'm in your debt, kind Sir, and I'd like to repay your kindness by offering you three wishes."

"Why, thank you," said Paddy, "I wish I had a bottle of whiskey in me hand right now!"

No sooner had he spoken than a bottle of whiskey appeared in his hand, and he unscrewed the cap and took a swig.

"You've two more wishes," said the leprechaun, "and I don't want to rush you but I must be getting along soon."

"OK, then," said Paddy, "I wish this bottle would never get empty!"

"Done!" said the leprechaun, and sure enough, every time Paddy had another swig, the bottle filled itself up again.

"And for your third wish?" enquired the leprechaun.

"Begorrah," slurred Paddy, waving the magic bottle around, "I think I'll have another one of these."

An Irishman is sitting at a bar and is already three sheets to the wind. He asks the barman for another Guinness and throws it down. He has six more beers until he can hardly speak. He says to the barman, "Gghive me shone shmore." The barman refuses to serve him.

The Irishman gets livid and says to the man, "You llllisthen chere buddy. I'm payin ya goooood smoneys to have a Guinessh, you gives me one rightsh f**king shnow!"

The barman doesn't want any trouble so he gives him another Guinness. The drunk downs it and demands another. Again wanting no trouble, the barman decides to make a deal with him.

So he says to the Irishman, "Listen here lad, I'll only give you another one on three conditions – you must do three things for me."

The drunk says, "Okay, just give me a f**king beer."

The barman begins his commands, "First, see that bouncer over there? He's new and I need you to pick a fight with him and test him out." (The bouncer is absolutely huge and the barman knows that the drunk stands no chance.)

The drunk stands up from the bar, walks up to the bouncer, looks up and lays him out with one punch, returns to the bar and demands a beer.

The barman says, "Wait, there are two more things you must do next – there's a guard dog in the back all chained up who's got a tooth ache. He's a vicious animal and doesn't let anyone near him. You must go and pull his bad tooth. Then when you're done with that, I've got a sister upstairs who's ugly as sin and will never get fucked as long as she lives. She's feeling pretty bad about herself. Go upstairs and give her a good time. When you're done with them, come back here and I'll treat you for the rest of the day to all the brew you want."

The drunk gets up, goes in the backroom and all you could hear was the dog squealing.

The drunk comes back to the bar all sweaty and says, "Okay, so whersh your shishter with the bad tooth?"

Brenda O'Malley is home as usual, making dinner, when Tim Finnegan arrives at her door.

"Brenda, may I come in?" he asks. "I've somethin' to tell ya."

"Of course you can come in, you're always welcome, Tim. But where's me husband, Seamus?"

"That's what I'm here to be tellin' ya, Brenda. There was an accident down at the brewery..."

"Oh, God no!" cries Brenda. "Please don't tell me..."

"I must, Brenda. Seamus is dead and gone. I'm sorry."

Brenda reached a hand out to her side, found the arm of the rocking chair by the fireplace, pulled the chair to her and collapsed into it. She wept for many minutes. Finally she looked up at Tim: "Tell me, how did it happen, Tim?"

"T'was terrible, Brenda. He fell into a vat of Guinness Stout and drowned."

"Oh dear Jesus! But you must tell me true, Tim. Did he at least go quickly?"

"Well, no Brenda. I'm sorry to say, it wasn't quick at all."

"Oh, dear God, me poor Seamus!"

"Fact is, he got out three times to piss."

A man stumbles up to the only other patron in a bar and asks if he could buy him a drink. "Why, of course," comes the reply.

The first man then asks: "Where are you from?"

"I'm from Ireland," replies the second man.

The first man responds, "You don't say, I'm from Ireland too! Let's have another round to Ireland."

"Of course," replies the second man.

Curious, the first man then asks: "Where in Ireland are you from?"

"Dublin," comes the reply.

"I can't believe it," says the first man. "I'm from Dublin too! Let's have another drink to Dublin."

"Of course," replies the second man.

Curiosity again strikes and the first man asks, "What school did you go to?"

"Saint Mary's," replies the second man, "I graduated in '62."

"This is unbelievable!", the first man says. "I went to Saint Mary's and I graduated in '62, too!"

About that time, in comes one of the regulars and sits down at the bar. "What's been going on?" he asks the barman.

"Nothing much," replies the barman. "The O'Mally twins are drunk again."

An Irishman has been at a pub all night, drinking. The barman finally says that the bar is closed. So he stands up to leave and falls flat on his face.

He decides that he'll crawl outside and get some fresh air and maybe that will sober him up. Once outside he stands up and falls flat on his face. So he crawls home and at the door stands up and falls flat on his face. He crawls through the door and up the stairs.

When he reaches his bed he tries one more time to stand up. This time he falls right into bed and is immediately asleep. He wakes up the next morning with his wife standing over him, shouting at him.

"So, you've been out drinking again!"

"How did you know?" he asks.

"The pub called, you left your wheelchair there again."

An old Irishman moved from his village to another closer to the hospital as he was beginning to age a bit.

He went into the local pub and ordered three pints of Guinness Stout. When he drank, he drank one sip from the first, the second, and then the third. After drinking like this for a while, he finally finished all three glasses. He took them up to the bartender for a refill.

The bartender said, "Ya know me friend, if ya were to drink this beer one glass at a time it would be a might fresher and bit more enjoyable."

The man replied, "Ay, a reckon so, but me two brothers and I agreed to drink our beer this way ever since they emigrated to the United States. It's our way of remembrin' one another."

The bartender replied, "Aw now, that makes sense."

The man became a regular and one day came in and ordered only two beers. He drank those in his normal fashion, sipping from each glass one at a time. The other locals and the bartender were quiet and hushed.

When the man came up for a refill the bartender said, "Me friend I am sorry about ya los'n ya brother."

The man replied, "Aw naw, it's noth'n like that, it's just that I stopped drink'n."

McAteer arrived at Heathrow Airport and wandered about the terminal with tears streaming down his cheeks. An airline employee asked him if he was already homesick.

"No," replied McAteer, "I've lost all me luggage!"

"How did that happen?" the man asked.

"The cork fell out," said the Irishman.

REALLY
WICKED
DRINKING
JOKES

An attractive young lady walked into a working class bar and said to everyone in the bar that she had a riddle for them to answer. If no-one could answer the riddle everyone had to buy her a beer but if someone were able to answer it they would get to have sex with her.

The lady said,

"If my pussy should sail out to sea how would you get it back for me?"

No-one in the bar could give her an answer, so everyone there bought her a beer.

The next night she went to a middle-class bar with the same offer. Again no-one had an answer for her, so everyone bought her a beer.

The next night she entered an upper-class bar, again with the same riddle and the same offer. After a couple of minutes an old man stood up and said,

"If that time should come to pass I'd tie my balls onto my ass, use my cock as an oar and float your pussy back to shore."

She was an attractive barmaid so he slapped a tenner on the bar and said, "I bet I can keep an eye on this drink while I go to the gents."

She knew the gents' loo was around the corner, so she accepted the bet. He took his glass eye out, placed it beside the glass and went to the gents.

"Betcha I can bite my own ear," he challenged. The bet was accepted and he took out his false teeth and nipped his ear. Once more he scooped up the money.

"Okay," he said, "I'll give you a chance to win your money back. I bet I can make love to you so tenderly you won't feel a thing." Now that was one thing she really did know about. So she accepted the bet. He lifted her skirt and away they went.

"I can feel you," she cried.

"Oh well," he said, "You win some, you lose some!"

There was a black man, a white man, and a Mexican sitting in a bar, all drunk. The black guy says to the white guy, "I bet you my cock is bigger than yours."

The white guy says, "No way, mine is bigger than yours."

The Mexican, overhearing the conversation, comes over and says, "No, mine is bigger than both of yours," and starts laughing.

All three of them carried on drinking and arguing.

The white guy comes up with a solution. He says, "We'll all pull our cocks out and put them on the table. That way, we'll see whose is bigger."

All of them agreed and took their cocks out. While they were looking at each other's cocks and comparing them, one of them said, "So, whose is bigger?" None of them could figure it out because they couldn't see straight and were drunk.

While they were standing there, a gay guy walks in and says, "Ohhh Buffet."

A man walks into a New York bar and asks the bartender for a shot of forty-year-old Scotch. Not wanting to go down to the basement and deplete his supply of the rare and expensive liquor, the bartender pours a shot of ten-year-old Scotch and figures that his customer won't be able to tell the difference.

The man downs the Scotch and says, "Hey, that Scotch is only ten-years-old. I specifically asked for forty-year-old Scotch."

Amazed, the bartender reaches into a locked cabinet underneath the bar and pulls out a bottle of twenty-year-old Scotch and pours the man a shot.

The customer drinks it down and says, "That was twenty-year-old Scotch. I asked for forty-year-old Scotch."

So the bartender goes into the back room and brings out a bottle of thirty-year-old Scotch and pours the customer a drink. By now a small crowd has gathered around the man and is watching anxiously as he downs the latest drink. Once again the man states the true age of the Scotch and repeats his original request.

The bartender can hold off no longer and disappears into the cellar to get a bottle of prime forty-year-old Scotch.

As the bartender returns with the drink, an old drunk, who had been watching the proceedings with interest, leaves the bar and returns with a full shot glass of his own.

The customer downs the Scotch and says, "Now this is forty-year-old Scotch!" The crowd applauds his discriminating palate.

"I bet you think you're real smart," slurs the drunk. "Here take a swig of this."

Rising to the challenge, the man takes the glass and downs the drink in one swallow. Immediately, he chokes and spits out the liquid on the bar floor.

"My God!" he exclaims. "That's piss!"

"Great guess," says the drunk. "Now tell me how old I am."

SIMPLE

MISTAKES

A white horse walks into a pub, pulls up a stool, and orders a pint of lager. The landlord serves him his beer and says, "You know, we have a drink named after you."

To which the white horse replies, "What, Eric?"

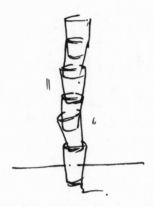

A heavy-drinking New Yorker saw a sign that said "Drink Canada Dry" ... so he went there.

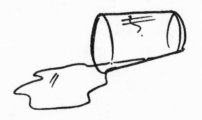

Two drunks met in a bar.

"What's the date, Jimmy?" asked one.

"Dunno," replied Jimmy.

"Well, look at that newspaper in your pocket."

"No use," said Jimmy. "It's yesterday's."

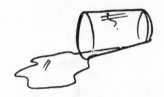

Two men were in a pub, doing some heavy boozing. They were drinking doubles and triples, buying rounds and generally having a good time. When asked why they were celebrating, they boasted that they had just finished a jigsaw puzzle and it had only taken them two months.

"TWO MONTHS," exclaimed the barman, "That absurd. It shouldn't take anywhere near that long."

"Well," said one of the men, "The box said two to four years."

The fire engine careered around the corner and whizzed off up the road, bells clanging, just after a drunk staggered out of a pub. He promptly started chasing after it, but collapsed, exhausted and weeping after only a few hundred yards. "All right," he sobbed, "You can keep your rotten ice lollies!"

There were two deaf drunks travelling on the tube:

First drunk: "Is this Wembley?"

Second drunk: "No, it's Thursday."

First drunk: "So am I, let's get out and have one!"

A man walked into a pub and demanded to be served a drink called 'Less'.

"I've never heard of it." said the barmaid.

"You must have heard of it!" insisted the man

"Well, we don't stock it, I'm afraid. Is 'Less' a new, foreign beer or something? Where did you hear about it?" asked the barmaid.

"I don't know exactly what it is," replied the man, "but my doctor insists that I drink 'Less'."

A six-year-old boy walks into a pub, climbs up onto a stool and says, "Give me a Scotch on the rocks."

"You're just a child!" the barmaid says. "Do you want to get me into trouble?"

"Maybe later," the boy replies. "In the meantime, I'll have that drink."

In a small, rural village, the local drunk is weaving his way up the main street. The local vicar, a rather harsh man, famed for his puritanical views, is watching his progress with a disdainful eye. The drunk spots him and lurches over. "Your Holynesh, you're my besht mate. How the hell are you?"

This combination of drunkenness and profanity is too much for the vicar who explodes, "Drunk! And on a Sunday!"

"Your shecret's shafe with me, Reverend. To tell the truth, I've had a couple of quick ones myself."

Two young men are sitting in a disco, both pretty drunk, when one of them notices a beautiful woman standing on her own in the corner. "Wow!" he says to his mate, "I'd love to dansh with her."

"Go and ashk her, then, don't be a chicken." said the mate.

So the first man goes over and says, "Excushe me, Mish, would you like to dansh with me?"

Seeing that he is totally drunk and rather

inexperienced, the woman says, "I'm sorry –
right now I'm concentrating on matrimony and
I'd rather sit than dance."

The young man returns to his mate looking
really put down.

"What did she say, then?" he asks.

"She said she's constipated on macaroni and
would rather shit in her pants," came the reply.

At the end of his shift, the Aussie barman turns on the TV in the London pub where he's working to catch the highlights of the day's play in the Ashes.

There is only one drinker in the pub and he becomes equally engrossed in the game. When the Aussie pace bowler bowls out one of the England openers, the drinker puts it down to luck. When, with his next ball, the same bowler clean bowls the incoming batsman, the drinker is outraged at the 'fluke'.

Such is his indignation that he bets the barman £10 that the bowler won't get a hat-trick. The barman has seen that part of the game earlier and accepts the bet, knowing full well that the bowler does get his hat trick.

They watch the third ball, the drinker bellows in disbelief and hands over the tenner to the guilt-stricken barman.

"No, I can't take your money, mate. I watched it live this afternoon."

"So did I," replied the drinker. "I just didn't think he'd able to pull it off twice in a row."

An Englishman, a Scotsman and an Irishman were on a flight crossing the Atlantic when the plane got into trouble. The captain made an announcement to the effect that everyone should stay calm but at further notice should prepare themselves for a crash landing. Immediately there were several requests for alcohol from the frightened passengers. As there was really no time to serve them, the stewards started to hand out bottles from the duty free trolly. The Englishman requested a bottle of gin and drank it neat. The Scotsman thought he'd done pretty well to secure not one but two bottles of Scottish whisky and was soon blotto. However, when it came to the Irishman he requested to sleep with the black stewardess who was asking him what bottle he wanted. At first she demurred but then thought she might as well oblige if she was going to die anyway so they went off to the back of the plane and started to make love. "Why did you want to sleep with me rather than get drunk with your friends?" she asked at one point. To which the Irishman replied, "Well I've heard that the only part of a plane that survives a crash is the black box. Now I'm in it."

A man walks into a pub and notices he's the only one there, apart from the barman, who's on the phone. The barman signals him that he'll be with him in a minute. The man nods, sits on a stool and waits to be served.

Suddenly, he hears a little voice say, "Hello, you're looking rather smart today. New suit?"

The man looks around but can't see anyone else in the place. He hears the voice again. "Seriously... THAT is a fabulous tie, chum!" The man looks around again and still doesn't see anyone.

"Hello?" he asks. "Is someone speaking to me?"

"Absolutely! I just have to say you look marvellous! Have you lost weight?"

A crowd of other tiny voices suddenly chorused in agreement. The man realizes now that these voices are coming from a bowl of peanuts on the bar in front of him. He stares at them as the barman finally hangs up and comes to serve his only customer.

"What'll you have?" asks the barman.

"What?... Oh, a pint of bitter, I suppose," mutters the man, still staring at the peanuts. He finally looks up at the barman drawing his pint.

"What about these nuts?" he asks.

The barman brings the man's pint over and sets it before him.

"Oh, the nuts? They're complimentary!"

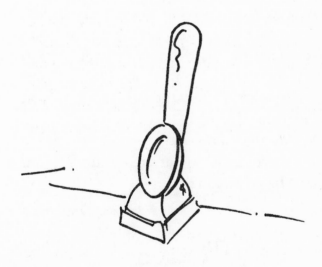

A man is minding his own business in his local pub, drinking a pint of beer, when a gorgeous looking girl comes in, sits down beside him and gives him a stunning smile. Just as he's thinking up his opening line, she says in a loud, indignant voice that everyone can hear, "Your place? Certainly not!" and she gets to her feet and moves to the other end of the bar.

He sits there feeling completely em-barrassed, imagining what everyone is thinking of him and wondering how he can ever live this down. After a while the girl comes back and sits down next to him again. In a low voice she says, "I'm so sorry about that. I'm a psychology student and I'm conducting an experiment to discover how people react to unexpected stressful situations. Please accept my sincere apologies and let me buy you another drink."

Quickly the man stands up and says at the top of his voice, "One hundred pounds? You must be bloody joking!"

A man walks into a bar and sits down next to a sailor whose head is about the size of an orange. The man and the sailor begin to talk and after ten minutes, curiosity got the better of the man and he asked, "How did you get that tiny head of yours?" And so the sailor began.....

"When I was in the navy, my ship sank and I was the only survivor. I swam to a nearby deserted isle and, when I arrived, I heard a woman yelling for help.

I found a mermaid stranded on the beach. She was the most beautiful woman I ever saw! I carried her to the water and she said, 'For your generosity I will grant you three wishes.'

Of course, I accepted.

'MY FIRST WISH,' I said, 'Will be to be FILTHY RICH.' A huge box of jewels appeared on the sand.

'MY SECOND WISH will be to get home safely.' And a golden yacht with beautiful women on it appeared on the horizon, headed for the island.

'MY THIRD WISH will be to make love to you,' I said.

'Well,' she replied, 'as you can see, I'm not really built for that sort of thing.'

'Then how about just a little head?'."

A punk with a multicoloured mohawk, spiky hairdo goes into a pub to have a couple of beers. After a while he notices an old man at the other end of the bar, staring at him. Every time he looks up this man is still staring.

Finally he can't take it any more, so he goes over to the man and says, "Why are you staring at me? Haven't you ever done anything weird in your life?"

The old man says, "I certainly have done some weird things in my life. As a matter of fact, I had sex with a peacock once, and I was wondering if you were my son!"

111

A juggler, driving to his next performance, was stopped by the police.

"What are those knives doing in your car?" asked the officer.

" I juggle them in my act," he replied.

"Oh yes?" says the policeman. "Let's see you do it."

So the juggler starts tossing and juggling the knives.

A man driving by sees this and says, "God, am I glad I stopped drinking. Look at the test they're making you do now!"

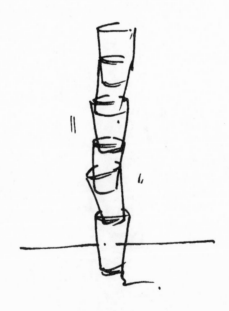

LAW AND ORDER

One day while on patrol, a policeman pulled over a car for speeding. He went up to the car and asked the driver to roll down her window. The first thing he noticed, apart from the fancy red sports car, was how attractive the driver was. Long blonde hair, fantastic figure, she really was the bee's knees.

"I've pulled you over for speeding, madam. Could I see your licence please?" said the policeman.

"What's a licence? replied the blonde, instantly giving away the fact she was as thick as a plank.

"It's usually in your wallet," replied the officer. After fumbling for a few minutes, the girl managed to find it.

"Now can I see your insurance details?" asks the copper.

"Insurance details? What are they?" she asked.

"They're usually in the glove compartment," said the copper, growing impatient. After some more fumbling, she found her insurance details.

"I'll be back in a minute," said the copper and walked back to his car. He radioed in to

run a check on the woman's details and, after a few moments the control room came back to him.

"Is this woman driving a red sports car?" asked the voice over the radio.

"Yes," said the copper.

"Is she a really sexy looking blonde?"

"Uh, yes," replied the copper.

"In that case, give her back her licence and insurance and drop your trousers."

"WHAT?" shrieked the copper, "I can't do that."

"Trust me, just do it," said the man in the control room.

So the policeman goes back to the car, gives the girl back her documents and drops his trousers. The blonde looks down and sighs, "Oh, no... not ANOTHER breathalyser."

Two old drunks come stumbling out of a pub and start pissing in a nearby garden. A policeman comes along and takes them in on charges of indecent exposure. Writing up the charge, the policeman says to the first drunk, "What's your address?" But the man is so drunk he can't remember and says, "I don't know."

Irritated, the policeman turns to the second drunk, "Well, where do you live?"

"I live next door to him." comes the reply.

Late one night the police were following a car. The driver was driving immaculately, never exceeding the speed limit, giving all the correct signals and even being courteous to other drivers.

Eventually the police car came alongside him, indicating that he should pull over. "Good evening, Sir," the officer said, "Don't be alarmed, you aren't in any trouble – we just wanted to compliment you on your exemplary driving."

"Thank you, officer," replied the driver. "I always make a point of driving carefully at night, especially when I've had a few pints."

Two policemen walked over to a drunk lying on the beach.

"We're looking for a drowned man," they said.

"You don't shay," said the surprised man. "Whatcha want one for?"

A rabbi and a priest were involved in a car accident, and it was a bad one. Both cars were totally demolished but, amazingly, neither of the men were hurt. After they crawled out of the wrecks, the rabbi noticed the priest's collar and said, "Well, you're a priest and I'm a rabbi and just look at our cars. They are both write-offs but we've escaped unhurt. It must be God's will. He must have intended us to meet, become friends and live alongside each other in peace for the rest of our days."

"I absolutely agree with you." the priest replied. "this is certainly a sign from God."

"And just look at this," the rabbi continued, "here's another miracle! My car is totalled but this bottle of kosher wine didn't break. Surely God wants us to celebrate our good fortune with a drink." And he handed the bottle of wine to the priest who took a few, big swigs and handed the bottle back. The rabbi put the cork back in and threw the bottle as far away as he could into the woods.

"Aren't you having any?" asked the priest.

"No," replied the rabbi. "I think I'll wait for the police."

An Irishman was brought up before the judge. "Why were you drunk?" the judge asked.

"I was on a train with bad companions." replied the Irishman. "Four teetotallers."

"But they are the best company you could keep!" exclaimed the judge.

"I don't think so, your Honour. I had a bottle of whisky about my person and I had to drink it all by myself."

A policeman sees a car weaving all over the road and pulls it over. He walks up to the car and can smell alcohol on the breath of the attractive lady driver.

He says, "I'm going to have to give you a breathalyser test to see if you are under the influence of alcohol."

She blows into the bag and he walks back to the police car. After a couple of minutes he returns and says, "It looks like you've had a couple of stiff ones."

"Good gracious," she exclaims, "you mean it shows that too?"

The policeman was on the witness stand.

"I could see him in the middle of the road on his hands and knees."

"Your honour," interrupted the lawyer. "Just because a man is in the middle of the road on his hands and knees at midnight is no sign that he is drunk."

"What the counsel for the defence says is quite true," agreed the policeman. "But the defendant was trying to roll up the white line."

HEALTH WARNINGS

The doctor was trying very hard to persuade Josh to give up drinking. "Have you ever noticed a cactus plant?" he asked the heavy boozer. "If you pour water round its roots it thrives, turns greener and grows bigger. If, however, you pour alcohol on it, what happens? It shrivels, turns brown, and dies. Doesn't this teach you anything, Josh?"

"Yes, Doctor," said Josh, "it teaches me that if I want a large cactus growing in my stomach, I should drink plenty of water!"

Suggestions for when they put health warnings on alcohol...

WARNING: Consumption of alcohol is a major factor in dancing like an idiot.

WARNING: Consumption of alcohol may lead you to believe that ex-lovers are really dying for you to telephone them at four in the morning.

WARNING: Consumption of alcohol may cause you to tell the same boring story over and over again until your friends want to smash your head in.

WARNING: Consumption of alcohol may cause you to thay shings like thish.

WARNING: Consumption of alcohol may cause you to tell your boss what you really think about him while photocopying your backside at the office Christmas party.

WARNING: Consumption of alcohol may leave you wondering what on earth happened to your knickers anyway.

WARNING: Consumption of alcohol is the leading cause of inexplicable rug burn on the forehead.

WARNING: Consumption of alcohol may create the illusion that you are tougher, more handsome, and smarter than some really, really huge biker bloke named 'Big Al'.

THE COMPUTER FREAK'S GUIDE TO BEERS...

DOS Beer: Requires you to use your own can opener, and requires you to read the directions carefully before opening the can. Originally only came in an 8-oz. can, but now comes in a 16-oz. can. However, the can is divided into 8 compartments of 2 oz. each, which have to be accessed separately. Soon to be discontinued, although a lot of people are going to keep drinking it after it's no longer available.

MAC Beer: At first, came only a 16-oz. can, but now comes in a 32-oz. can. Considered by many to be a "light" beer. All the cans look identical. When you take one from the fridge, it opens itself. The ingredients list is not on the can. If you call to ask about the ingredients, you are told that "you don't need to know." A notice on the side reminds you to drag your empties to the wastebasket. Anyone drinking it regularly will insist it is THE best beer. Even if they have never tried any other beer.

Windows 3.1 Beer: The world's most popular. Comes in a 16-oz. can that looks a lot like Mac Beer's. Requires that you already own a DOS Beer. Claims that it allows you to drink several DOS Beers simultaneously, but in reality you can only drink a few of them, very slowly, especially slowly if you are drinking the Windows Beer at the same time. Sometimes, for apparently no reason, a can of Windows Beer will explode when you open it.

OS/2 Beer: Comes in a 32-oz can. This does allow you to drink several DOS Beers simultaneously. Allows you to drink Windows 3.1 Beer simultaneously too, but somewhat slower. Advertises that its cans won't explode when you open them, even if you shake them up. You never really see anyone drinking OS/2 Beer, but the manufacturer (International Beer Manufacturing) claims that 9 million six-packs have been sold.

Windows 95 Beer: The can looks a lot like Mac Beer's can, but tastes more like Windows 3.1 Beer. It comes in 32-oz. cans, but when you look inside, the cans only have 16 oz. of beer in them. Most people will probably keep drinking Windows 3.1 Beer until their friends try Windows 95 Beer and say they like it. The ingredients list, when you look at the small print, has some of the same ingredients that come in DOS beer, even though the manufacturer claims that this is an entirely new brew.

Windows NT Beer: Comes in 32-oz. cans, but you can only buy it by the lorry load. This causes most people to have to go out and buy bigger refrigerators. The can looks just like Windows 3.1 Beer's, but the company promises to change the can to look just like Windows 95 Beer's. Touted as an "industrial strength" beer, and suggested only for use in bars.

Unix Beer: Comes in several different brands, in cans ranging from 8 oz. to 64 oz. Drinkers of Unix Beer display fierce brand loyalty, even though they claim that all the different brands taste almost identical. Sometimes the pop-tops break off when you try to open them, so you have to have your own can opener around for those occasions. In that case you either need a complete set of instructions, or a friend who has been drinking Unix Beer for several years.

Amiga Beer: The company has gone out of business, but their recipe has been picked up by some weird German company, so now this beer will be an import. This beer never really sold very well because the original manufacturer didn't understand marketing. Like Unix Beer, Amiga Beer fans are an extremely loyal and loud group. It originally came in a 16-oz. can, but now comes in 32-oz. cans too. When this can was originally introduced, it appeared flashy and colourful, but the design hasn't changed much over the years, so it appears dated now. Critics of this beer claim that it is only meant for watching TV anyway.

VMS Beer: Requires minimal user interaction, except for popping the top and sipping. However cans have been known on occasion to explode, or contain extremely un-beer-like contents.

Best drunk in high pressure development environments. When you call the manufacturer for the list of ingredients, you're told that is proprietary and you are referred to an unknown listing in manuals published by the MOD.

Rumours are that this was once listed in the GP's' Desk Reference as a tranquillizer, but no one can claim to have actually seen it.

REALLY WICKED FOOTBALL JOKES

A man arrives at the gates of heaven, where St Peter greets him and says, "Before I can let you enter I must ask you what you have done in your life that was particularly good."

The man racks his brains for a few minutes and then admits to St Peter that he hasn't done anything particularly good in his life.

"Well," says St Peter, "have you done anything particularly brave in your life?"

"Yes, I have," replies the man proudly.

St Peter asks the man to give an account of his bravery.

So the man explains, "I was refereeing this important match between Liverpool and Everton at Anfield. The score was nil-nil and there was only one more minute of play to go in the second half when I awarded a penalty against Liverpool at the Kop end."

"Yes," responded St Peter, "I agree that was a real act of bravery. Can you perhaps tell me when this took place?"

"Certainly," the man replied, "about three minutes ago."

A footballer died and arrived at the gates of heaven where an angel awaited him. "Now," said the angel, "before you enter here, is there anything that happened to you on earth upon which you would like your mind set at rest?"

The footballer thought for a moment and then said: "There is one matter, I belonged to the famous St Mirren Club and one cup final when we were playing the Rangers, I scored a goal which I am sure was off-side. It won us the match and the cup, but I've always been troubled about it".

"Oh," replied the angel, "We know all about that goal up here. It was perfectly right, so you can banish your doubts."

"Oh, thank you, St Peter," said the footballer. The angel replied: "But I'm not St Peter, you know." "Then who are you?" Asked the footballer. "St Mirren," came the reply.

Fixed to a wall in Liverpool in the mid-1960's was a Baptist poster which read, "What would you do if Jesus returned among us?"

Underneath the poster someone had written, "Move St. John to inside left."

A group of Catholic priests were due to play a group of rabbis in an important inter-faith game. A few days before the match, disaster struck. The Catholic team's star player broke his ankle and the doctor said he wouldn't be able to play again for at least two months.

"What are we going to do? moaned Father Durnford.

"Well," said Father Thomas, "it so happens that Alan Shearer is a good friend of mine. We could ask him to play for us."

"But that wouldn't be ethical, now would it?" said Father Durnford.

"No, but if we called him Father Shearer, no one need know," replied Father Thomas.

Eventually Father Durnford agreed to let this devious plan go ahead but then, as luck would have it, he was suddenly called away on official Church business and was unable to watch the match. As soon as he could, he phoned Father Thomas for the result.

"I'm afraid they beat us, five-one," said Father Thomas.

"But how could that happen?" queried Father Durnford. "We had Father Shearer in our team."

"Yes," said Father Thomas, "but they had Rabbi Ince and Rabbi Gascoigne playing for them."

A great footballer was tragically killed and arriving at heaven's gates, he came face-to-face with the angel on duty.

"Is there any reason why you shouldn't be allowed to enter the kingdom of heaven?" asked the angel.

"Well," said the footballer, "there was one time when I cheated in a major international football game."

"I see," said the angel, "tell me about it."

"Well," said the footballer, "I was playing for Wales against France and I used my hand to push the ball past a French defender. The referee didn't see it and I went on to score."

"And what was the final score?" asked the angel.

"That was the only goal," said the footballer, "We won one-nil."

"Well, that's not too serious. I think we can let you in," said the angel.

"Oh terrific!" exclaimed the footballer, "It's been on my mind for years. Thanks a lot, St. Peter."

"That's OK," said the angel, ushering the footballer in, "and by the way, it's St. Peter's day off today, I'm St. David."

The Devil was constantly challenging St Peter to a game of soccer, but St Peter refused, until one day while walking around heaven he discovered that quite a number of international footballers had entered the 'pearly gates'.

"I think I'll arrange to play that soccer game," said St Peter to the Devil. "We have a great number of international soccer stars in heaven at the moment from which to select a winning team."

"You'll lose, you'll lose!" taunted the Devil. "What makes you so sure we'll lose?" enquired St Peter. "Because," laughed the Devil, "we have all the referees down here."

The goalkeeper threw a party after his team won the league championship. As a special honour, he asked the manager to say grace before they sat down to dinner.

Finishing up the short prayer, the manager said, "... and we thank you, Lord, in the name of the Father, the Son, and the goalie host."

Three old football fans are in a church, praying for their teams. The first one asks, "Oh Lord when will England next win the World Cup?"

God Replies, "In the next five years."

"But I'll be dead by then," says the man.

The second one asks, "Oh Lord, when will Forest next win the European Cup?"

The Good Lord answers, "In the next ten years."

"But I'll be dead by then," says the man.

The third one asks, "Oh Lord when will Derby win the Premier League?".

God answers, "I'll be dead by then!"

LIVE

ON

AIR

The following quotes show just how over-excited some of our favourite football commentators can become...

"Barcelona... a club with a stadium that seats 120,000 people. And they're all here in Newcastle tonight!"

"Ronaldo is always very close to being either onside or offside."

"We were a little bit outnumbered there, it was two against two."

"Julian Dicks is everywhere, it's like they've got eleven Dicks on the field."

"If England are going to win this match, they're going to have to score a goal."

"You weigh up the pros and cons and try to put them into chronological order."

"Robert Lee was able to do some running on his groin for the first time."

"I never comment on referees and I'm not going to break the habit of a lifetime for that prat."

"I'm not a believer in luck..... but I do believe you need it."

"What will you do when you leave football, Jack... will you stay in football?"

"Unfortunately, we keep kicking ourselves in the foot."

"Celtic were at one time nine points ahead, but somewhere along the road, their ship went off the rails."

"I've got a gut feeling in my stomach..."

"The new West Stand casts a giant shadow over the entire pitch, even on a sunny day."

"I would not say he [David Ginola] is the best left-winger in the Premiership, but there are none better."

"Johnson has revelled in the 'hole' behind Dwight Yorke..."

"An inch or two either side of the post and that would have been a goal."

"Both sides have scored a couple of goals, and both sides have conceded a couple of goals."

"You don't score 64 goals in 86 games at the highest level without being able to score goals."

"What's it like being in Bethlehem, the place where Christmas began? I suppose it's like seeing Ian Wright at Arsenal..."

"And we all know that in football if you stand still you go backwards..."

"I was saying the other day, how often the most vulnerable area for goalies is between their legs..."

"The lad got over-excited when he saw the whites of the goal post's eyes."

"If you can't stand the heat in the dressing-room, get out of the kitchen."

"The lads really ran their socks into the ground."

"He [Brian Laudrup] wasn't just facing one defender — he was facing one at the front and one at the back as well."

"It's now 1-1, an exact reversal of the score on Saturday."

"...but Arsenal are quick to credit Bergkamp with laying on 75% of their nine goals."

"an excellent player, but he [Ian Wright] does have a black side."

"We say 'educated left foot', of course, there are many players with educated right foots."

"That's twice now he [Terry Phelan] has got between himself and the goal."

"Mark Hughes at his very best: he loves to feel people right behind him..."

"Gary always weighed up his options, especially when he had no choice."

"We threw our dice into the ring and turned up trumps."

"And I suppose they [Spurs] are nearer to being out of the FA Cup now than any other time since the first half of this season, when they weren't ever in it anyway."

"...and he crosses the line with the ball almost mesmerically tied to his foot with a ball of string..."

"I never make predictions and I never will."

"And there's Ray Clemence looking as cool as ever out in the cold."

"...and the news from Guadalajara, where the temperature is 96 degrees, is that Falcao is warming up."

"If history is going to repeat itself I should think we can expect the same thing again."

"The Uruguayans are losing no time in making a meal around the referee."

"I think that was a moment of cool panic there."

"Beckenbauer really has gambled all his eggs."

"Celtic manager Davie Hay still has a fresh pair of legs up his sleeve."

"I spent four indifferent years at Goodison Park, but they were great years."

"Souness gave Fleck a second chance and he grabbed it with both feet."

"They have missed so many chances they must be wringing their heads in shame."

"It's headed away by John Clark, using his head."

"Tottenham are trying tonight to become the first London team to win this Cup. The last team to do so was the 1973 Spurs side."

"He's very fast and if he gets a yard ahead of himself nobody will catch him."

"The shot from Laws was precise but wide."

"The game is balanced in Arsenal's favour."

"Merseyside derbies usually last 90 minutes and I'm sure today's won't be any different."

"Many clubs have a question mark in the shape of an axe-head hanging over them."

"Tottenham have impressed me. They haven't thrown in the towel even though they have been under the gun."

"You have got to miss them to score sometimes."

"Dumbarton player Steve McCahill has limped off with a badly cut forehead."

"A contract on a piece of paper, saying you want to leave, is like a piece of paper saying you want to leave."

"And I honestly believe we can go all the way to Wembley... unless somebody knocks us out."

"It was that game that put the Everton ship back on the road."

"And Arsenal now have plenty of time to dictate the last few seconds."

"Bobby Robson must be thinking of throwing some fresh legs on."

"What makes this game so delightful is that when both teams get the ball they are attacking their opponent's goal."

"That's football, Mike, Northern Ireland have had several chances and haven't scored but England have had no chances and scored twice. and so they have not been able to improve their 100% record."

"In terms of the Richter Scale this defeat was a force eight gale."

"In comparison, there's no comparison."

"I would also think that the action replay showed it to be worse than it actually was."

"Mirandinha will have more shots this afternoon than both sides put together."

"Newcastle, of course, unbeaten in their last five wins."

"Football's not like an electric light. You can't just flick the switch and change from quick to slow."

"Certain people are FOR me and certain people are PRO me."

"I'm going to make a prediction – it could go either way."

"And with 4 minutes gone, the score is already 0-0."

"They have got their feet on the ground and if they stay that way they will go places."

"Being naturally right-footed he doesn't often chance his arm with his left foot."

"Strangely, in slow motion replay, the ball seemed to hang in the air for even longer."

"What I said to them at half-time would be unprintable on the radio."

"If we played like this every week, we wouldn't be so inconsistent."

"If there weren't such a thing as football, we'd all be frustrated footballers."

"He's one of those footballers whose brains are in his head."

"The crowd think that Todd handled the ball.... they must have seen something that nobody else did."

"I can see the carrot at the end of the tunnel."

"They compare Steve McManaman to Steve Highway and he's nothing like him, but I can see why – it's because he's a bit different."

"Glenn Hoddle hasn't been the Hoddle we know. Neither has Bryan Robson."

"There's no way Ryan Giggs is another George Best. He's another Ryan Giggs."

"The only thing I have in common with George Best is that we come from the same place, play for the same club, and were discovered by the same man."

"For those of you watching in black and white, Spurs are in the all-yellow strip."

"I don't think there is anybody bigger or smaller than Maradona."

"Jimmy: "Don't sit on the fence Terry, what chance do you think Germany has got of getting through?
Terry: "I think it's 50-50."

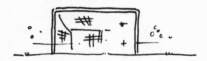

"I was disappointed to leave Spurs, but quite pleased I did."

INJURY TIME

Derek played football with his mates every Sunday afternoon in the local park. His right knee had been giving him trouble for some time, but recently the pain had been even worse than usual so he decided to see the doctor.

When he arrived at the surgery, the nurse told him he could see the doctor in 15 minutes but first he would have to give a urine sample. Derek said that it seemed crazy to give a urine sample to help solve his knee problem. However the nurse insisted, so eventually Derek complied. A quarter of an hour later he was ushered in to see the doctor.

"So, that knee is giving you trouble again, eh?" said the doctor almost immediately.

"The nurse must have told you then," said Derek, wondering how the doctor knew.

"No. It was in your urine analysis," the doctor replied. "We've got a new urology machine which can diagnose every physical condition with complete accuracy."

Derek didn't believe a word of it, but nevertheless he agreed to provide another urine sample on a check-up visit.

A few days later, Derek was sitting at the

kitchen table with his wife and teenage daughter. He was telling them about this ridiculous machine, when he decided to have a little fun with the doctor. He peed into the sample bottle, as did his wife and daughter. Then he had the idea of giving even more 'spice' to the proceedings. He added a few drops of motor oil to the bottle and finally had a wank and put a few drops of semen in with it too. He returned to the doctor's surgery, shook the bottle and handed it to the nurse.

This time the urine analysis took half an hour. Finally Derek was ushered in to see the doctor. The doctor looked at him and said, "I'm afraid I've got some bad news for you. Your daughter's pregnant, your wife's got V.D., your car's about to break down and if you don't stop wanking, that knee's going to get even worse."

A football player had dislocated his shoulder in a nasty challenge, and was still screaming in agony when they got him to hospital.

"For Heaven's sake," said the doctor, "you're supposed to be a big, tough defender. There's a woman having a baby next door and she's not making anything like the noise that you are."

"That's as may be," wailed the footballer, "but, in her case, nobody's trying to push anything back in."

The top scorer of a Premier League team was tragically killed in a car accident. Seeing an opportunity for glory, the reserve striker went to see the manager. "How about me taking his place?" he asked.

"Well, I'm not sure about that," said the manager, "we'll have to speak to the undertaker first."

After a visit to the doctor, Joe Bloggs, the city team's centre forward dropped in to his local pub for a quick one. "What's up mate?" asked his friend Brian, "you look worried."

"Yes, I am," Joe replied. "I've just been to the doctor's and he told me I can't play football."

"Oh, really?" said Brian. "He's seen you play too then, has he?"

A full back with a reputation for being a really hard man on the pitch was sent off during a match. Returning to the changing room, he had a terrible leg. It was covered in cuts and bruises and had a massive gash from the top of the thigh to the knee. He had no idea whose it was.

In the middle of the defensive wall at a free kick, the left back took the ball right in the crotch and he passed out from the pain. When he woke up he found himself in the local hospital. Though still in pain, he asked the doctor, "Doc, is it bad? Will I be able to play again?"

"Yes, you should be able to," replied the doctor.

"Oh, great. So I can play for my club again?" said the man, feeling much relieved.

"Well, just as long as they've got a women's team," said the doctor.

REALLY WICKED SCOTTISH JOKES

A man went to the pub with his great dane, and when he arrived he left the dog outside, securely tied to a post. A few minutes later, a Scotsman arrived.

Scotsman: "Is that your dog outside?"

First Man: "Yes. What of it?"

Scotsman: "Well, I think my dog's gone an killed him?"

First Man: "Whatever kind of dog have you got that could kill a great dane?"

Scotsman: "I hae a Chihuahua"

First Man: "But how could a Chihuahua kill a great dane?"

Scotsman: "The wee tyke must hae got stuck in his throat!"

The Society of the Paranormal was having a convention in town and there were several hundred delegates attending. The president of the society was at the podium delivering the opening address to all who were there in body and in spirit, and he asked the question:

"Which of you has had the occasion to see a ghost?"

About 40 people raised their hands and the speaker asked them, "Which of you has had the occasion to speak with a ghost?"

This time about 30 delegates raised their hands.

The speaker then posed a third question,

"Which of you has had the occasion to have actually touched a ghost?" in answer to which about ten hands were waved about. The speaker paused for a moment, and then delivered yet another query,

"Which of you has had the occasion to have sex with a ghost?" In the far corner of the auditorium a lone hand was raised. The speaker then said, "Would the usher please escort that individual, with his hand raised, to the podium? I simply must enquire further."

After a few moments delay the individual,

who incidentally turned out to be a wee Scotsman in full kilt and highland regalia, was brought forward to the stage.

When the Scot arrived at the podium, the speaker asked him, "Well, Sir, tell us what it was like to have sex with a ghost," to which the man replied, "Ghost? Laddie, I thought ye said goat."

THE

CANNY

SCOT

Q. What's the difference between a Scotsman and a coconut?
A. You can always get a drink out of a coconut.

Q. Why do the Scots have double glazed windows?
A. So that their kids can't hear the ice cream vans.

Q. How are the Scots and crime alike?
A. Neither of them pay.

Q. Why do Scottish people refuse to buy refrigerators?
A. They don't believe that the light will go out when you close the door.

Q. Why don't Scotsmen ever have coffee the way they like it?

A. Well, they like it with two lumps of sugar, but if they drink it at home, they only take one lump, and if they drink it while visiting, they always take three lumps.

Scotsman to taxi driver: "How much is it to the airport?"

Taxi driver: "That'll be £5.20."

Scotsman: "And what would it be just for the luggage?"

Taxi driver: "Luggage? that's free, of course!"

Scotsman: "Ok. You take the luggage. I'll just walk!"

Jock was in terrible trouble. His business had gone under, and he was in a serious financial mess. He was so desperate, he decided to turn to God for help, and went to the kirk to pray.

"Oh God! Ye've got tae help me! I've lost mae business and if I don't get some money I'll be losing mae hoose as well. Please let me win the lottery."

Lottery night came, and someone else won.

Jock went back to the kirk.

"Oh God! Please let me win the lottery! I've lost my business, mae hoose and noo I've lost mae car!"

Lottery night came and still Jock had no luck.

Back to the kirk.

"God! Why hae ye forsaken me? I've lost mae business, mae hoose, mae car – and mae wife and bairns are starving! I've never asked ye for anything else before, so why don't ye help me? Why don't ye let me win the lottery?"

At that moment there was a blinding flash of light as the heavens opened. And Jock was confronted with the voice of God himself.

"Jock! Why don't you meet me halfway on this one! Buy a f**king ticket!"

Robbie Macphee went into a barber's shop and asked the barber the price of a haircut.

"Two pounds," said the barber.

"How much is a shave?" asked Macphee.

"One pound," said the barber.

"Shave my head," said Macphee.

You have to be very careful about stereotyping the Scots as mean. There was a letter in the paper the other day from an angry Glasgwegian. It said, "If you print any more jokes about Scotsmen, I shall have to stop borrowing your paper."

Did you hear the one about the Scotsman who died of a broken heart? He was fed up with reading jokes about how mean the Scots are, so he went into his nearest pub and ordered a round for everyone in it.

"That's very kind of you, sir," said the publican. "There must be 50 people in here. I didn't know you Scots were so generous."

The Scotsman was visiting London for the day and found himself in Soho where he called upon a prostitute. After he had spent a couple of hours in bed with her, he gave her two thousand pounds.

"That's incredibly generous of you!" the girl gasped. "No punter has ever paid me so much money before. And yet, from your accent I'd say you were a Scotsman."

"Aye, you're right." the Scotsman replied.

So which part of Scotland are you from?"

"From Edinburgh." the Scotsman replied.

"That's a coincidence," the girl said, "My Dad works in Edinburgh."

"I know," said the Scotsman. "And when he heard I was coming down to London he asked

me to bring you a share of his Lottery winnings
- two thousand pounds."

Johnson married the most shapely girl in the
office, and all his mates envied him, in particular
an unmarried young Scot who said one day, "Ye
ken, I'd give a hundred pounds to smack the
pretty bottom of yon wee wife o'yours."

Johnson was furious and went home raging
to his wife about it. But the wife had Scottish
blood too, and she said, "Well you know, the
furniture isn't paid for yet, and I could do with
a fur coat. What's a few smacks on the bottom,
when all's said and done?"

Eventually she wore her husband down and
finally he was obliged to tell Jock that he could
smack his wife's bare bottom for a hundred
pounds, but only on the condition that he had
to be there while it happened. Then he could
make sure there was no funny business.

So the three of them got together on a
Saturday night in the Johnson's bedroom and
the blushing wife pulled down her knickers,
stepped out of them and bent over the bed.

Jock lifted her skirt up and started to gently
stroke her bottom saying, "What beautiful

curves! What a delicate shade of pink! What charming dimples! how lovely and firm it is!" And all the while he was stroking and caressing while Johnson was becoming more and more enraged.

When Jock suddenly produced a camera from his pocket and started taking photographs, Johnson finally shouted, "Get on with it, will you? Smack her right now or the whole thing's off!"

"Och no!" said Jock, "I could never bring myself to smack such a beautiful bottom as this one. And besides, it would cost me a hundred pounds if I did!"

Have you heard the one about the Grand Canyon having been started by a Scotsman who lost a penny in a ditch?

A Scotsman is a man who goes to a wedding with a broom and brings home the rice for dinner.

Tea Time in Scotland:

"Dad!" called the little boy, "There's boiling water coming out of the radiator!"

"Don't waste it!" shouted his Dad in reply. "Throw in a tea bag."

Scotsman: A man who stays at home and lets his mind wander.

My uncle is a Scotsman. He runs his toothpaste tube through the wringer but my auntie has hers run over by a bus.

Jock was out of cigarettes so he decided to ask his friend Sandy for a match. When he had got the match he searched his pockets and said, "I seem to have forgotten my cigarettes."

"In that case you won't be needing the match," replied Sandy.

The Scotsman comes to his friend in tears. "My beautiful comb," he cries. "I broke a tooth on it and now I can't use it any more. What am I going to do? Now I'll have to buy another one."

"Well," said his friend, "you don't need to buy another just because you lost one tooth on your comb."

"But you don't understand," said the Scotsman, "it was the last tooth."

Mike is living in Glasgow and drops in on his friend, Jimmy, who lives down the road.

When he arrives Jimmy is stripping all the wallpaper off the walls in his living room.

"Oh, you're decorating," says Mike.

"Nay, laddie," says Jimmy, "I'm moving."

THE
BRAW
KILT

A Scotsman, wearing a kilt, was walking down a country path after finishing off a considerable amount of whisky at a local pub. As he staggered down the road, he felt quite sleepy and decided to take a nap with his back against a tree.

As he slept, two young lasses walked down the road and heard the Scotsman snoring loudly. They saw him, and one said, "I've always wondered what a Scotsman wears under his kilt." She boldly walked over to the sleeping man, raised his kilt, and saw what nature had provided him at his birth.

Her friend said, "Well, he has solved a great mystery for us. He must be rewarded!" So, she took a blue ribbon from her hair, and gently tied it around what nature had provided the Scotsman, and the two walked away.

Some time later, the Scotsman was awakened by the call of nature, and walked around to the other side of the tree to relieve himself. He raised his kilt...and saw where the blue ribbon was tied.

After several moments of bewilderment, the Scotsman said,"I dinna know where y'been laddie...but it's nice ta' know y'won first prize!"

Sandy McTavish was wandering around the local department store when he spotted a bolt of the McTavish clan tartan at a spectacularly low price. As his own kilt was six years old and very shabby, he was delighted, and approached the shop assistant.

"Lassie! I'd like a yard and a half of that McTavish tartan. I'll be needing a new kilt."

" Of course, sir. Could you show me which tartan you want?"

Sandy walked over to the display table and showed her the plaid.

"Sorry sir, that tartan only comes in three-yard lengths."

"Ye dinna understand, lassie! I just need a yard and a half!"

"I'm very sorry sir! But the plaid comes in three yard lengths. Why don't you use a yard and a half to make your kilt, and use the other half to make a scarf for your girlfriend?"

It was clear to Sandy that he was going to have to buy the whole three yards if he was going to get a new kilt.

"All right, lassie! I'll take the three yards!"

He took the plaid home and made a new kilt for himself and a scarf for his girl friend. He was so pleased with the kilt, that he decided to go over to her house to show it off. He'd keep the scarf as a surprise for later.

He'd forgotten that in the six years since he'd worn his old kilt he'd lost over two stone in weight. But he'd used the same pattern for the new one. As he was rushing to his girl friend's house, the kilt slipped over his hips and was gone. In his excitement he didn't even notice. He got to her door and knocked.

She saw him from the window and opened the front door. As she did, he threw open his coat and said:

"Well! Hae de ye like that?"

She stared for a moment and replied "I like it just fine, Sandy!"

"Aye, lassie, and there's another yard and a half ye'll be gettin' for Christmas!"

I've just washed my kilt and I can't do a fling with it.

Tourist: "Is anything worn under that kilt?"

Scotsman: "No, everything's in perfect working order."

"So you belong to a Scottish regiment. Do you have the right to bear arms?"

"Of course, and we have the right to bare legs."

Mac was courting a wee lassie, and this wee lassie had a wee flat, but Jock could never get any further than the doorstep. Every night he would take her home and ask, "Can I come in for a wee while, Mary?"

And Mary always replied, "Nae, nae, Jock, I can see the glint in yer eye."

Jock realized that this 'glint in the eye' business was his undoing, so one night, as he took Mary towards the door of her flat, he sneakily put on a pair of dark glasses.

"Can I come in for a wee while, Mary?" he asked.

"Nae, nae, Jock." she replied.

"But Mary!" Jock exclaimed, "Ye canna see the glint in me eye!"

"Nae, nae, Jock," said Mary, "but I can see the tilt o' yer kilt!"

How do you tell a Scotsman's clan?

You put your hand up his kilt and if you feel a couple of quarter pounders, you'll know he's a Macdonald.

An American tourist sees a Scotsman in a kilt. She has always been curious to know what is worn under a kilt so, summoning up her courage, she asks him.

The Scotsman replies that, if she really wants to know, she is welcome to feel under his kilt in order to satisfy her curiosity. So she gingerly places her hand under his kilt... "Oh, it's gruesome," she shrieks, quickly removing her hand.

"Aye," replies the Scotsman, "and if you'd like to try it again, you'll find it's gruesome more."

The Director of the Scottish Tartans Museum, Dr Hamish MacDonald was in America. An old lady fixed her gaze on his 17th century sporran and asked, "What, exactly, do you keep in your scrotum?"

THE
BONNY
PIPES

"I just found out why the bagpipes make the Scotsmen brave in war."

"Why is that?"

"They'd rather die than have to hear them."

A Scotsman was seriously ill in hospital. His doctors were very afraid that this was to be the end of him, since there was nothing that they could do to make him healthy.

His doctor came to his bedside and asked him if there was anything he could do to make him comfortable during his final hours.

"If I could hear the pipes one more time, it would make me very happy, doctor."

So the doctor arranged for a piper to come into the ward and play for the dying man.

As soon as the Scot heard the pipes the colour came back into his cheeks, his eyes became bright, his breathing became easier and he got up and danced around the ward. He was completely cured.

Later, while recounting the story over lunch

the doctor confessed that this was a miracle cure that he really couldn't explain.

"I was amazed!" he said "When the pipes began to play, the man was completely cured. The only problem though was that two Englishmen who'd just come in for checkups died on the spot!"

There are many theories about the bagpipes, otherwise known as the missing link between music and noise.

The truth is that they were given to the Scots by the Irish as a joke....but the Scots haven't seen the joke yet!

OTHER BOOKS
IN THE SERIES:

THE
TRULY
TERRIBLE
JOKE BOOK

THE
ABSOLUTELY
FRIGHTFUL
JOKE BOOK